AF406719

DEVOURED BY PAIN

an illustrated collection of poetry

A.X. SALVO

ABOUT THE AUTHOR

A.X. Salvo is the author of the international bestselling poetry collections *The Teeth Of The World Are Sharp*, *The Muse Of Love & Pain*, and *Devoured*.

Salvo's writings and art have appeared in *USA Today*, *MISC*, *Studio Visit Magazine*, *Bete Noir*, *The Adroit Journal*, and *The Anthologist*. Salvo is also the recipient of a Vermont Studio Center grant for Poetry.

www.axsalvo.com
TikTok & Instagram: @axsalvo

APERITIF

"A fiendish love... an unearthly love... those who feel such a love are numbed to their very souls by this mysterious pleasure while they struggle with endless frustration, censured by the pangs of conscience of their boundless crime."

— **Junji Ito**

For Junji

POEMS

HURT

Without you

I am weightless

Without you

my mouth

is dry and hungry

as a withered beggar

Without you

my mind

is madness

my passion

dissolved

These thoughts

are injuries

I cannot sustain

NO TIME FOR CONVERSATION

I

I just want to be used

no time for conversation

I don't need a friend now

I need a lover

One

Brutal

Lover

This has nothing

to do with love

or friendship

or even lust

this is about

absolving my sins

with your skin

this is about me

burying my guilt

deeper and deeper within you

each thrust deeper than the last

I want you to force

your tongue past

closed angry lips

choke me until I'm blue

slap me until I'm red

ride me till my eyes

go pearl white, bite

me until I bleed, scratch

into the flesh of my back with

scarlet fingernails, lick

the length of my collar bone

I want to be left

with bruises everywhere

my face, neck, chest,

thighs and cock, I want you

to grab fists full of

my long coffee brown hair and

pull and pull and pull

until I'm forced to yell

moan

squeal

cry

II

I've taken

beatings before

I've given

a fair share of them myself

I can take

all kinds of punishment: I've been

punched, choked, stabbed and

burned and kicked and pushed

face to the piss and shit wet ground

I have scars

some muddy some clean

that would welcome more

This transaction

would cost

Nothing

III

Can you please

mistreat me?

This life has grown

tiresome

I just need a little

abuse before bed, it helps

me sleep, you know

And when you're finished

turn off the heat

turn off the lights

take all the blankets

when you leave me

lavender

bare

frigid

tattered

in that topaz darkness

Because this

will always be about

the benefits of frustration

self loathing, and a little

abuse

these are my burdens

these are my faults

this is my mess

never yours

SELFISH

I'll never

shake

the shame

of keeping you

all to myself

NOTHING

Once you looked upon me

with the eyes of an architect

wanting nothing

but to build great things

your eyes are now

filled with arson

wanting nothing

but to watch

my face burn

TREES AND DEMONS

Shake my tree of life and

watch the serpents fall

rearrange me until I'm saved

until I'm safe

consider this a plea for help

turn this demon into a saint

paint my red sins white

paint my black soul blue

teach me the algorithms

to life and love

for I know nothing of either

TOUCH

Tonight

No amount of liquor

can bring me love

No amount of love

can intoxicate me

And

not even

the touch of tree bark

can make me feel a part

of this world

DIRT

I can already feel

the dirt of yesterday's

disappointment

soiling my today

I'm beginning to feel like

everyone's whore

Worst part being

I'm the one

paying for everything

DROWNING

Will you meet me

at the bottom of the ocean?

The currents your hands make

reach me before

your fingers reach the

flesh of my face

before your lips land

on my eyes and

bring the world into focus

This consolation, however brief,

is the light that warms this abyss

that divides the

shadow from the good

This love is what binds

the wolf to the tree, what

quiets those apparitions of guilt

the deafening ghosts' cry

What a fool I've been

living life, believing I could win

this war at my core

this search for epiphany, meaning

in a world whose language

I can speak

but will never understand

My past still

clings to my skin, the stink

I cannot wash, but may

one day purge with

your milk, your nourishment

At the bottom, perhaps

we will find a little peace

the quiet we seek

with every breath

Until then, I ask and ask and

fling my questions into the abyss

waiting for the moment

my destiny is revealed

What will galvanize my being?

What will be the catalyst

that will make my self implode?

Revealing a better structure

a less flawed edifice

a man deserving of

a great woman

Is this hope valid,

or will my sins find me here?

reach me here?

These fears

cut my courage

into slivers, and I

can do nothing but wait

with you at my side

cradling my face

in your small hands

at the bottom of the ocean

4AM

A man can

only go so

long without a lover

Sadness will make him mad

Madness will make him sadder still

And above all

this

remains clear

I

do not belong here

LUST JUNKIES

I

A girl once left me

with many

marks, cuts, and bruises

her emerald eyes were always

hard and petulant just as

the life and mind of a

recovering addict should be

She took it all

out on me, gave me

all the rage

she could summon

She wrapped tattooed palms around

my lithe strained neck

shoved elbows into the blades

of my shoulders

force fed me

bare breasts

bony limbs

smoky lips

and a pierced

fuchsia clit

II

After I finally tore

free from her hold, I

buried my shovel into her soil, I

proved I was

just as guilty

just as shameless

just as vicious

I dug and dug and dug and dug

daring, desperate and dying

to find something underneath the girl

underneath me

She wailed and made a scene of it

an outpour of wicked pleasure

she whispered: I'm crying

because it feels too good

but I knew she cried

because she thought

she didn't deserve to feel good

because there's no such thing

as feeling too good

III

She'd always say:

how her thighs were too thick

her lips too thin

freckles too many

voice too small

eyes too shy

and I always

proved her wrong

She cut crimson diagonals

over the skin of my ribs

with dirty crooked nails

gripped me with a

violence leaving

violet fingerprint phantoms

over the translucent flesh of my waist

That emblazoned trail of

the narcotic bliss we felt

Another high

tugging on our blue cables

filling us with the promise

of a momentary fix

Lust junkies

pallid and livid

always looking for the back door

always coming down

slippery steps

Moans became whimpers

we had hurt each other

somehow

I had gone too far

inside her

risked too much

beside her

just to hide our rage — our grief

somehow

GOOD

I wondered of

how many men you've left

marooned

on fruitless islands

I cried until

my tears turned

the dirt

beneath my feet

into mud and charred

antlered devils

with maroon skins

burst through the ground

to slather us our sex

with soil and love and smut

Sin never felt

so goddamned good

DEEP GREEN

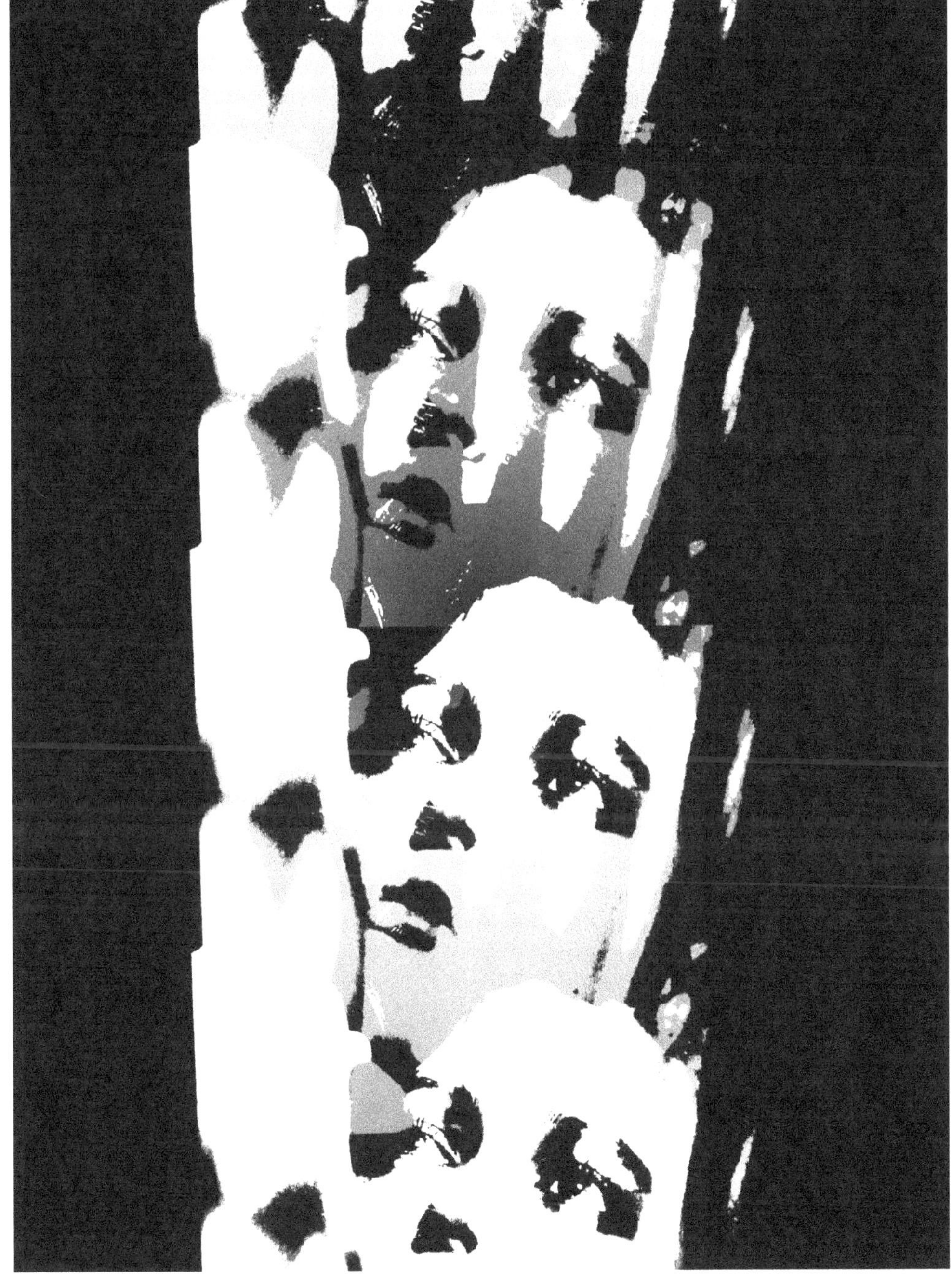

Oh, I beg you

can I follow?

You're my fever

running high

running deep

running wild

And across the river

at the pier

in the twilight

your beauty glows

sad, glorious, and

in full bloom

like a vast orange grove

engulfed in flame

And after midnight

when your madness

bursts into full bloom

and you unravel like a

starling lost in a storm

I'll follow...

I'll follow...

I'll follow you

down into the ocean

I will gladly leap

once again

into that same

Cold

Dark

Deep

Green

ABSENCE

Your presence

made such

a deep impression

on me that

your absence

has left me

cavernous

WHERE YOU SLEEP

I

I lost you

in a forest of blue green

flames

I don't know

how to find you

So many years have passed

since you've visited

I remember the raw

umber of your eyes,

but not the shape

I remember the angry

red of your hair,

but not the smell

I remember the quiet

pink of your mouth,

but not the laughter

I remember the bloodless

white of your skin,

but not the taste

Try as I might,

I no longer

dream of you.

I lost

my place again,

my home again,

my friend again

And now,

only Death and Death alone knows

who looks after you and

where you sleep

II

But I know where and

how your tomb lies

how quiet the black earth has become

I don't regret

ignoring your grave

all these years

it doesn't matter

where we buried you

you were never here

Death is stubborn

she refuses to take me

to your bedside

until I satisfy

needs and deeds

unknown

Until then,

I will do my best

to keep these unsteady hands

and their wanting

for the golden dagger

that will bring me

back

to you

NOISE

I thought

you were sent to

soothe a smoldered soul

I thought

you understood

I'm translucent and fragile

as rice paper

You treated my bones

like the branches

you tread upon

when you stepped away

from our home

and into that seething sun

Now

I do nothing, but

sleep and dream

sleep and dream

sleep and

dream guillotine dreams

To sever myself

from this mind and its

severe thoughts with

One

Quick

Cut

Asleep, yet awake

running, yet still

I burn

without flame

whispers are now screams

everything is noise

SMALL THINGS

I am surrounded

in a crowded Manhattan pub

full of single souls

with their bright teeth and

trim shapes and long legs

To hell with them

I'm in the corner, slung over

a wooden stool, avoiding

all conversation

The women here stare at me

their eyes say

they want to touch me,

but I don't want their hands

I need yours

I don't want anyone

to touch me but you

So I drink and

fool myself into forgetting

Desperate to find a way to bury you

I search my mind for the shovel

I distract it, seeking redemption in

the small things I do:

I throw colors against a canvas

I water my plants

I conjure a poem

call my father

check my email

beat my face

into the bathroom tiles

iron pants

I will never wear

jerk my cock

bite my nails

drink coffee

sweep the floor

argue with a cashier

walk through the bad

parts of town after dark

drink whiskey

jerk my cock

drink more whiskey

listen to Radiohead

fight strangers

weep with

all the lights off

Sleep

But it's not enough

It never is

GHOSTS

It's so strange

isn't it?

How people appear

and vanish

from our lives?

WILL

Having gone so long

without your song

without your fury

It's as if

you've died

and

I am unsure if

I can continue

to exist

in a world where

you do not

But I will try

my love

I

will

try

DEVOUR

Much like the

blood red berries

that stained the

skin of your

pale and perfect fingers

I nourish you as

you devour me

THIS IS FOR YOU

I'd give a rib to make another you

I'd break another bone

I'd beat another man

I'd do that too

I'd set fire to cities

I'd blacken pale angels

I'd deal with the Devil

I'd do that too

I'd carve myself another face

I'd wrap myself in wire

I'd make myself expire

I'd do that too

If it would bring us closer

Make me closer

To another you

WARM MACHINES

I

Sifting through the wreckage,

the tousled stranger

finds wire

finds metals

finds threads

of light

fine ovals

of shadow

stitches, staples, tape

bolts, batteries, clay

Forms

a man

forms

a woman

We are

such

warm machines

such

warm machines

II

We wake

shin skin torn

our shells devastated and muddy

covered in night

in a field of blood-

orange leaves

Our blue metal is starting to show

everyone will soon get suspicious

we may have to start

running soon

furious as exposed spies

I stare at the sky

I say:

those stars don't look

quite right tonight

eyes glimmer and do not

merely watch

they whisper

the darkness purrs

I plead:

we should go away for a while,

my love

but you never listen

III

You look beyond the field

at the hanging garden

impressed by

the strange animals

filling and drinking

their bejeweled cups of wine

surrounded by

great, gray stone pillars

I pull at you and say:

this is nothing but theater

this is no Babylon

You look out

at the silent animals

to find

a crowd

of smiling still

faces like foxes,

bodies of angels

clothed in the coldest light

and fire

questions

Why can't I do that?

what is happiness?

why can't I be like them?

how long must we wait?

when

will we be like them?

and after

a long stretch of quiet

I say:

never

We're just

warm machines

such

warm machines

We will never

eat how they eat

speak how they speak

think how they think

breathe how they breathe

love how they love

fuck how they fuck

That's why you sleep

and can't stand

to be around

too many

of them for

too long

Why you rarely leave

this field of dead red leaves

Because

ours,

ours is

a colder kind of love

a stranger spell of magic

a warmer form of logic

ruled by zeros and ones

and not

the constant threat

of oblivion

we cannot understand

fear

Death does not shake us

funerals are not events

We can never die

because

we were never truly alive

We're just

warm machines

such

warm machines

IV

I am an inferior model

made of plastic and copper and tin

living barely on oil and coal

You...

you are awakened by and filled with

the sun

you are

made of gold and light and porcelain

I am

built from parts

used and mislabeled —

something is off

on

the inside

there are pieces missing

Can't you tell this by my gait?

(every move I make

sounds like

loose change

spilling 'round the bottom

of a bucket)

Made listless,

I'll still manage

love

somehow

I cannot bruise,

but I will bend and

most certainly rust

time is a

hell of a thing,

my love

V

Those goddamned animals,

you'd think

they would know better

than to come here

than to

touch

our crimson wires

linked to the

chambers

of hearts imperfect

Those goddamned animals

and their curious hands

We explode

blown back

into the hanging garden

We run

they chase

pull us apart

try to learn

what made us undead

try to steal

what keeps us awake

But

we use what we've learned

patterns, rhythms, algorithms

we use what we've learned

to survive, to live

but only as fugitives

(repeat after them)

If you say this

they'll believe that

Assimilated

we convince them that we are

one and the same and

for a moment

we find safety

in numbers

VI

Once

during your absence

someone touched

the wrong wire

a careless error

system corruption

severed connection

broken transmission

loss of communication

blank screens

phantom dreams

flickering imagery

My screams

became

your screams

a lifetime of nothing

became everything

we never wanted

Snow snuck into our lives

winter hid all the places

we found ourselves

Tongues were held

gradually

more than hands

No longer able to

process your affection

I finally recognize

how obsolete I've become

You say:

Don't you leave me here

Don't you want to find

where you belong?

Don't you want to find home?

With my back to you, I

face the distant wreckage

and say:

My love,

I have found home

You say:

Don't you dare leave me here

I stare

at the ravens above the wreckage

and say:

If I don't go now

someone will just

come and take me away

any way

I may never know

what manner of science or religion

governed his or her or its vision

But of this,

I am certain

If this is my end

and

you cannot go on

without me

Whoever

created us

made

two

terrible

mistakes

MORE POETRY

Thank you for supporting an independent artist and helping me do what I love.

Please take a moment to explore my other books:

The Teeth Of The World Are Sharp

An illustrated collection of dark art and poetry inspired by Edgar Allan Poe, Sylvia Plath, Neil Gaiman and the horror manga of Junji Ito. *The Teeth Of The World Are Sharp* explores trauma, abuse, death, grief, and loss. Each poem is carefully illustrated with haunting black and white drawings

Where I End And You Begin

In this fourth collection of poems, Salvo takes you deeper into the shadows and delivers another brutally emotional experience with even more of what readers loved from his bestselling book *The Teeth Of The World Are Sharp* with more than 150 pages of new poems and hauntingly beautiful black and white drawings that blend dark fantasy, myth, and horror.

The Muse Of Love & Pain

Blurring the lines of poetry and fiction, this blend of gothic verse and fable is an ode to anyone who has traveled through the darkest roads and deepest waters to find love.

Devoured By Pain

Devoured By Love is an exploration of beauty, truth, and vulnerability. Salvo revisits his second book *Devoured* in a new volume featuring over 100 pages of intimate love poems and illustrations.

Devoured [text only]

Devoured is an exploration of the pleasure and the pain that can only come from love. I wrote this book of poems for all the souls who wander with shattered hearts.

PROJECTS

Beautiful Shadows

An illustrated anthology of dark art and classical poetry that includes famous poems by Poe, Neruda, Frost, Keats, and many others!

Pretty Hate Machine

A macabre horror/sci-fi tale told from the monster's perspective. *Pretty Hate Machine* introduces us to the trials of Orion. The ruthless beast that stalks the streets of the dystopian Chaoxte in search of human prey.